From the Nile to the Euphrates
The Call of Faith and Citizenship

A Statement of
The Christian Academic Forum
for Citizenship in the Arab World[1]

First Edition

From the Nile to the Euphrates
The Call of Faith and Citizenship

A Statement of
The Christian Academic Forum
for Citizenship in the Arab World

ISBN :9781507633687

Printing press: Latin Patriarchate
Art direction : Diyar Publisher
Designer : Engred Anwar Al-Khoury

1. Christianity and politics 2.Arab Christians 3.Citzenship
4. Middle East politics 5. Public Theology

---

w w w . d i y a r . p s

1. Background and Aim of this Document:

1.1 Responding to an invitation from the Diyar Consortium[2] that has been inquiring into the subject of religion and state in the Middle East [3] since 2008, we, a group of Christian academicians and young graduates, supported by Muslim intellectuals and academics, gathered together to contemplate our common concerns and common destiny within the Arab world. More important, we sought to create a unifying vision to help us and our communities remain steadfast in our homelands while we work toward rebuilding our societies, so that we all may have life and have it abundantly.

1.2 We have developed this document[4] to express our assessment of the agonizing realities of the Arab world, and to formulate a vision for the future of which we dream and which we aspire to achieve. We are well aware that dreaming and/or wishful thinking is not enough to fulfill our hopes, and that in order to make our vision come true we must build it into viable and durable reality. Presenting this document as a diagnostic statement is thus not enough. Our aspiration rather is to offer it as a platform for Middle Eastern thought, communication and dialogue. Working together is of utmost importance[5]. In addition to this document, we have prepared a plan of action for the coming two years (2015 and 2016) that will guide the first steps for what we hope will become a Christian Middle Eastern movement that will bind rather than divide – an inclusive movement bringing people of different faiths and diverse religious orientations in our region together to produce a new model of dynamic and vibrant citizenship. Certain questions may arise in the reader's mind:

1.3 - First: Why "From the Nile to the Euphrates"?

1.3.1 Academics and intellectuals from six countries participated in constructing this document. They came from Egypt, Syria, Lebanon, Jordan, Palestine and Iraq. These six countries form the cradle of civilization. They also represent a geopolitical area that is unique in nature, but has been fragmented by the implant of the State of Israel into its heart. The structure of these countries differs from that of the Arab Gulf States, as well as from that of the countries of North Africa. Furthermore, this area is the birthplace of Christianity; and it is where the earliest Christians and Churches have been nurtured through the centuries.

1.3.2 While the phrase "From the Nile to the Euphrates" has been used historically to express the unity and special character of this area, it has at the same time been usurped and utilized as a code for gaining control and hegemony, beginning with the Sykes-Picot Agreement and leading up to and including the continuing, expansive claims of Zionism. We view the whole of this region as an entity that cannot soar high and freely like a bird without the power of both its wings, the Nile and the Euphrates, with Palestine as its beating heart.

1.4 - Second: What distinguishes this document from other documents?

1.4.1 Anyone reading the first part of the document (which makes up approximately 75% of the total text) will be presented with a well-researched analysis of the challenges that face our region. This analysis steers clear of kindled emotions, on the one hand, and of the logic of fear and worry, on the other. Rather, it dares to call the issues by their real names, based on objective and scientific studies. Such an academic approach is critical for understanding the concerns of the document; for we are convinced that we cannot understand our reality through the lens of subjective religious interpretations; and we know that there is no "religious solution" to the predicaments of our region. This document identifies ten existential issues, and underscores the importance of strategic planning for addressing the difficulties our area faces.

1.5 - Third: Why insert faith into this document? Should not doctrine and citizenship be separated?

1.5.1 In the first place, this document belongs appropriately to the category of what is called "public theology," which is a discipline that is engaged in many countries globally. This document, with the type of analysis it contains, forms the first attempt of its kind in the Middle East.

1.5.2 Secondly, the concept of citizenship has largely been the domain of sectors specializing in human rights and among groups that are primarily secular. The questions arising today are these: Can citizenship be inspired, motivated and upheld by faith? Can faith be a rafter to undergird full and responsible citizenship? Can our understanding of religion and religious interpretations be transcended in such a way to address social challenges and, at the same time, to revitalize religious discourse itself to be relevant to the issues of our times?

1.5.3 Thirdly, to disregard religious affiliation and belonging is to deny and exclude diversity! Today, more than ever before, we need to develop an understanding of what the document calls a "conscientious and dynamic faith." We need urgently to move away from a type of escapist religious spiritualization that tends more toward divination to an enlightened understanding of faith that will engage us socially to buttress active citizenship, and not be an impediment to involved citizenship. It is our hope too that a similar course of action can be taken by Muslims to help renew the Islamic religious discourse so as to render it more supportive of citizenship in a modern, civil state.

1.6 - Fourth: Why the Christian Academic Forum for Citizenship in the Arab World?

1.6.1 The answer is simple. The participants who worked on the development of this document see that there is an urgent need for a Christian academic forum that is not composed of institutional ecclesiastical leaders. For these have their own considerations and constraints. A forum of academic specialists is not subject to the ebb and flow of the region's political currents; instead, it is a research-based arena for free inquiry and exchange – in the manner of a "think tank" – and is the first of its kind in Christian circles. This forum will comprise a coterie of intellectuals from a number of Middle East universities, and will occasionally invite, as there may be need, other specialists from Western, African and Asian countries, to think and plan together – Christians, Muslims, people of other faiths, and even those who may not profess a particular religion, as free thought is not bound by creed.

1.6.2 The Forum has also ensured that it will not isolate itself in an ivory tower; hence, it has taken upon itself to work with university students and young graduates who are threatened by the ghost of high unemployment and thus may be tempted to emigrate. The Forum will seek ways to encourage young adults to remain firmly planted in their homelands and to be active and effective citizens.

1.6.3 As is clearly stated in this document, we do not claim that by means of a document or through this Forum we will change the map of the Middle East, nor do we pretend that we possess magical formulas or miracle prescriptions. Rather, we realize that solutions will not come unless they are the result of a social process fraught with labor pains – a process of gradual awareness based on peaceful resistance and a liberal movement of thought and attitudes. What we aim for here is to participate and make a positive contribution toward change – to believe, to work hard and to make things happen. We want to create a space for serious and objective discussion. Most saliently, we aim to think, to plan and to work together!

2. The Call of Faith and Citizenship

2.0 - The Issues Here and Now:

Anyone reflecting on the state of affairs of the Arab Middle East today finds an abundance of challenges. We have narrowed those challenges down to ten pivotal and critical issues affecting the destiny of our peoples. These major issues have been documented through extensive studies. They require our diligent and tireless response, and demand our most active participation girded by a conscious and dynamic faith.

2.1 - Issue #1: Religion and State[6]

2.1.1 As yet, there is no agreement on the best principles that should govern the relationship between religion and state. Furthermore, there is no single or unique system that may be considered ideal to form those relations. However, several patterns have emerged from the historical, cultural and social contexts of various countries. These patterns reflect the different models of how religion and state may relate as, for example, in the case of the United States in comparison to France, Germany to Sweden, India to Japan, or Malaysia to Indonesia.

2.1.2 Both religion and state are constructs of historical and social contexts; therefore, we realize that solutions will not be found by waving a magic wand, or through the import of Western or Eastern models. Instead, any viable solution must result through gradual and cumulative local social processes.

2.1.3 The relation between religion and state is neither static nor linear, but must be open and dynamic. The definitive word has not yet been spoken regarding what that relationship must be like; nor should we expect it ever to be spoken. Yet, so long as history continues to move forward, this subject constantly needs to evolve. In that respect, there will be no instant answers and no accurate, fixed formulas. Instead, viable alternatives, innovative initiatives and positive contributions need to be encouraged and could help establish healthy relations.

2.1.4 This region ranks last in the world for achieving a healthy relationship between religion and state[7]. This is evident in how the ruling regimes, as well as opposition movements, manipulate religion as a tool to exert control and unilateral authority, or, conversely, to overthrow them.

2.1.5 Establishing good and clear measures for an appropriate relationship between religion and state, based on the fundamental principle of mutual non-interference, is crucial for human progress and the development of the future of the Middle East. Disruption of a healthy balance in the relationship negatively affects the quality of life, hinders daily living, and impedes social progress. Furthermore, such disruption severely abridges the rights of minorities and women, and greatly narrows opportunities for youth. It also negates religious and intellectual pluralism, limits cultural diversity, and ultimately violates human dignity and freedom. Additionally, repressive religious systems inhibit production, squandering human potential rather than releasing and fulfilling it. Here, it must be emphasized that securing human dignity and well-being is at the core of religion and the ultimate raison d'être for statehood, raising this key question: Is it possible to create positive synergy between religion and state in a way that will ensure a better life for the individual in the Middle East?

2.2 - Issue # 2: Constitutions and the Rule of Law[8]

2.2.1 The rule of law remains absent in most countries of the Middle East, even though their societies are in direst need of it as a means of protection from political despotism on the one hand, and from tyrannical and repressive religious extremism that bans what it dislikes and legitimizes what suits its ambitions, on the other. The upholding of law is requisite for combating corruption within government, administration, and economy. It puts a halt to bribery, favoritism, nepotism, fraud, extortion and the misuse and abuse of power, not to mention forgery in elections, legislative and judicial manipulation, environmental tampering and scorn for the very sanctity of life.

2.2.2 In our Arab societies, there is a thin and dubious line between divine laws and human legislation. Religions, after all, can best serve as value resources for constitutions, whereas a legislative authority that is constituted by free and fair elections must frame conventional laws that are to be upheld by an independent judiciary. The application of such laws is to be carried out in a manner that is not influenced by self-interested patronage or selective advantage.

2.2.3 Most Arab constitutions still suffer from discrepancies and contradictions. Moreover, the mechanisms of their interpretation and implementation fall short of the required standards of constitutional justice. This calls for waging intensive campaigns of popular awareness and legal reform through the channels of education and the media on various levels. The peoples of this region yearn for, and look forward to, states that honor the rule of law where equal citizenship prevails based on equal rights and duties, making room for political, intellectual and cultural diversity. Our societies seek after states that do not discriminate on the basis of religion, creed, gender, race or color but that will establish legal guarantees of its citizens' rights and provide equal opportunities for all.

2.3 - Issue #3: Security of the Regime vs. Security of the Citizen[9]

2.3.1 In the decades following World War II and up to the present, most Arab states have given their prime attention to issues of "national security," which in reality has meant the security of the prevailing regime. With this priority, they have accumulated and stored huge arsenals of weaponry at the expense of human, social and economic development. Moreover, massive police surveillance devices and tapping apparatuses have taken control over most aspects of life. Instead of being concerned with the security of the citizen, national security has preoccupied itself primarily with the security of the ruler.

2.3.2 The "Arab Spring" has exposed the flaws of such flaccid regimes that no longer provide security either for the state or the citizen. Despite the tremendous investment in military equipment and security systems, the illiteracy rate in the Arab world has reached 36% [10], which is twice the global rate. Unemployment in our societies is the highest worldwide, making it necessary to create a staggering fifty million new jobs over the next decade. This reality presents the greatest challenge to our region's stability. It follows, therefore, that security priorities in the states of the region must be reordered in such a way as to focus on the citizen's security. That means the citizen's personal, physical and psychological well-being, including food security, the right to education and employment, the right to live in safety, free from fear and poverty, and the opportunity for creative production. Concomitantly, this also means that a state needs to build modern, progressive and impartial security systems that are capable of maintaining the unity, integrity and cohesiveness of the nation, while protecting minorities and the equal rights of all citizens.

2.4 - Issue #4: Management of Human and Natural Resources

2.4.1 The Middle East is a region that God has blessed with remarkable natural resources with almost unmatched and plentiful human, ethnic and cultural resources. Indeed the area is rich with natural resources including oil, minerals, natural gas, solar energy, wind, rivers, seas and lakes, deserts and fertile cropland. It also has an abundance of historical and archaeological heritage that is open to international tourism. And the region's unique location as a bridge connecting three continents gives it an unparalleled strategic geographic, economic and intercultural advantage that attests to a glorious past and affords a highly promising future.

2.4.2 What is lacking, however, are the skills to manage these resources efficiently and effectively, and the kind of comprehensive guidance and intensive instruction for the sustainable development of resources and the maintenance of the area's vitality, all of which are necessary for a better quality of life.

2.4.3 In the absence of competent management skills, prosperity turns to deprivation, people continue to suffer political repression and, amid growing divisions among clashing identities, the area's energies are wasted, its resources pillaged, its archaeological heritage plundered and its brain power estranged or drained. Daily existence is often a bitter endurance test, and people become aliens at home, caught up in ethnic, religious or political factions, or are marginalized as refugees victimized by wars, ethnic cleansing, genocidal campaigns or religious persecution.

2.4.4 There is no doubt that the implant of the State of Israel into the heart of the region has contributed significantly to its fragmentation and disintegration, and the diversion of vast resources toward militarization. Moreover, manipulative foreign policies by powerful nations have effectively shattered the national fabric and led to the emergence of deplorable extremist forces in most Arab countries since the end of the Second World War. The governments, peoples and religious bodies – including the Churches – of the area, however, cannot be exempt from responsibility.

2.4.5 The future of this area depends largely on learning the art of enhancing diversity and the skills of managing natural and human resources so as to transform the region from a state of destitution to a place for life with dignity, from being a wasteland to a thriving environment for nation building and human development; to save it from crumbling and to create expansive common spaces for innovation and empowerment. This region has enriched the world in ages past with faith and a wealth of knowledge, art, and civilization. It is time for it to be part of the movement of history toward the future – now, before it is too late.

2.5 - Issue #5: Women

2.5.1 Middle Eastern women suffer inequality vis-à-vis most rights and duties within all arenas and institutions of society including politics, the economy, health care, the media, civil status and family laws. International reports[11] confirm the existence of a clear imbalance between the sexes and a systematic gender gap based on outright discrimination and the prevalence of male traditions and unfair treatment, leading to female voicelessness, inadequate societal participation and general regression. For while women have achieved significant gains in these societies during and since the Arab awakening beginning in the latter part of the nineteenth century, most Arab countries still do not adhere to recognized international standards in relation to the protection of women's rights.

2.5.2 It is crucial, therefore, to persist vigorously in demanding the active participation of women in assuming leadership roles and in decision-making processes so that they may become effective contributors to the sustainable development of all aspects of society. If half of societies represented by their female populations are excluded from their move toward revitalization and growth, deterioration, impoverishment and crippling are inevitable, and the region will lag even farther behind in terms of genuine human progress.

2.5.3 Women have intrinsic and inalienable rights to participate in building their societies. The time has come to change all that has been and is unjust and non-constructive in order for women to enjoy their full humanity and maintain their dignity, and to attain their rights and fulfill their duties in an equal setting with men. Furthermore, it is imperative to develop new social, cultural and religious consciousness-raising vehicles to change prevailing attitudes so that women may assume their rightful, unabridged status and inclusive role in building society.

2.6 - Issue #6: Youth

2.6.1 Middle Eastern societies are typically characterized by their youthful populations. Indeed, youth make up more than half of the region's residential census. The sheer numbers of these young generations hold a unique potential; this is a challenge that should not be underestimated. A prime and overriding concern lies in the question: Can our societies adequately equip their youth academically, scientifically and professionally to become integrated in the process of nation-building, technological development and economic productivity? Or, will these young masses be added to the hordes of the idle, under- or unemployed, only to find themselves on the margins of society and history?[12]

2.6.2 Another formidable fact confronting our youth is the effect of globalization and the information revolution. A Middle Eastern young person is caught up in two worlds that are very different and, quite often, contradictory. Middle Eastern society imposes limitations that inhibit ambition and restrict movement. Society often sanctions whatever it pleases and condones what suits the moment. Yet today, there is another, virtual reality into which a young person can, at the click of a button, sail off to distant and alien shores, to lands perceived to flow with milk and honey, leaving him or her withering with hunger and thirst, dying inside from loneliness amid the crowds on the Arab street, consumed with emptiness and lost in the void of meaninglessness.

2.6.3 A third reality has to do with religious identity. Youth in today's Middle East are in a state of polarization. Some are recruited and steeped into camps of extreme religiosity; others are bored with religion and drift as far away as possible distance from it, while still others, unwilling to surrender their faith, are exasperated with dogma and repulsed with the mosques and churches.

2.6.4 These challenges that are thrust upon us impel us to work diligently on reforming the educational processes to capture the imagination and enthusiasm of our younger generations, and to invest in their minds to prepare them to meet the opportunities and demands that may be available to them and, as well, to embrace the open possibilities of global economic progress.

2.6.5 These profound realities also oblige us to empower the young to turn from being passive and helpless consumers in the new globalized world to being active, fluent and technologically competent, capable of full engagement with the worldwide web. Mastering this new global language will grant them access to the possibilities of a new universe, not just as a tool for communication but as a vehicle for dialogue that stimulates new horizons of thinking and learning, ultimately leading to raising the level of human civilization. In today's post-modern world, a new religious discourse must also develop, rooted deeply in genuine and purpose-driven faith to convey our youth from an environment of religious repression to the freedom of becoming "children of God."

2.7 - Issue #7: Human Dignity and the Quality of Life

2.7.1 The Universal Declaration of Human Rights is based on the principle of dignity and justice for all. It opens with the words, "…

the recognition of the inherent dignity and of the equal and inalienable rights of all members of the human family is the foundation of freedom, justice and peace in the world…" In this charter, the member states of the United Nations have reaffirmed their faith in fundamental human rights, and in the dignity and worth of every human individual.

2.7.2 Human dignity is inherent in all members of the human family, and is the foundation of equal and inalienable rights. Thus, it is the firm and immovable backbone of all the freedoms to which every human being is entitled, without distinction, on the basis of origin, gender, race, color, age or physical condition, whatever the nationality, language, culture, religion, doctrine, sect, place of residence, social, material, or political status. Everyone is entitled to freedom of thought, expression of opinion, freedom of conscience, and religious belief and practice, including the freedom to change one's religion or belief. Everyone has the right to security of person, and all are equal before just laws, and are entitled, equally, without discrimination, to legal protection under the banner of equal citizenship. No one shall be subjected to torture or to cruel, inhuman or degrading treatment or punishment. Everyone is entitled to a standard of living conducive to health and well-being for self and family, and to medical care and social services. Everyone, without distinction, is entitled to the right of work, to just and favorable employment conditions, to equal pay for equal work and to freedom from fear, oppression, persecution and scarcity. Everyone has the right to take part in the political process and to have equal access to the circles of law, authority, and an unbiased judiciary. Where are our Middle Eastern societies vis-à-vis those rights?

2.8 - Issue #8: Spirituality and Humane Culture
2.8.1 Those contemplating the situation of the Arab world today will invariably discern that, despite the proliferating numbers of those espousing religion in many of our countries, we are nevertheless

lacking a deep spirituality that is human and humane, nurtured by an awe of the Divine, committed to preserving the sanctity of life, principled to uphold the dignity of every child of Adam, and motivated to love and seek the well-being of neighbor, regardless of his / her identity, religion or belief. When these vital spiritual elements are absent, many resort in vain to seeking them in alternatives that have nothing to do with the essence of religion, and are in fact swept by superficial currents that lead to inhuman behavior.

2.8.2 In like manner, despite the growing numbers of university graduates in all specialties, we are nevertheless witnessing a remarkable and visible deterioration in civility and refined culture. The very soil that brought forth civilization has well-nigh become a dry wilderness in terms of urbanity, approximating prehistoric desert culture. Our region lacks an authentic spirituality and a refinement of cultural values that sanctify life, elevate human worth, and safeguard the needs of neighbor and society.

2. 9 - Issue #9: Reason in an Age of Irrationality

2.9.1 Most Arab societies live and move in an inverted world of surrealism and meta-realism. Religion is often mixed with other-worldliness, where God becomes a hook for superstition. Individuals turn passive and fatalistic; they cling to absent answers that override logic, willpower and work. Ours are societies that lack self-awareness and ignore scientific analysis which is necessary for understanding matters as they are rather than interpreting or justifying them as we guess, rationalize, or dream them to be. There are among us astute, sound and vocal religious leaders who are champions of rationality[13] in this age of extremist ideologies. They combat extremism and speak out against incitement, religious coercion, expulsion from homelands, terror and killing. But they are all too few. In our societies, no adequate strategies have been established to raise awareness relative to the foundations of sound citizenship, or to issues concerning the environment, health or education. Indeed, the lack of such efforts has kept us with closed mindsets amid the technological boom of civilization. We now have the responsibility to open the gates of reason and to create paths to a wise and enlightened faith that is not threatened by rational thought, sound logic, or scientific discovery[14]. Failing that, our nations can never rise, or find any hope in the future.

2.10 - Issue #10: The Need for a Unifying Vision

2.10.1 Currently, the Arab world is staring at a bleak horizon, and may be enduring the most difficult period in its modern history. There are no apparent easy solutions, nor any foreseeable deliverance. Consequently, many are afflicted with despair; frustration drives some toward emigration, others to resort to religious fundamentalism, while still others indulge in escapist consumerism. Today, our region is in need of investing in steadfast hope that is accompanied by serious and diligent work. The greatest challenge confronting us, in the face of our wretched state of polarization, fragmentation and loss, is a purposeful and unifying vision to bind us together toward an open and promising destiny.

2.10.2 That vision must go beyond realism without overlooking reality; it must be comprehensive without ignoring or dismissing the component parts; it must be hopeful, ambitious, lively, productive and fruitful. For a vision stripped of serious commitment, hard work and the capacity to bear fruit is nothing but a rosy dream.

3. Our Christian, Human and National Role

3.1 In light of the preceding, we deem it most fitting to focus on our Christian, human, and national roles in addressing these urgent challenges confronting our societies. We want to mobilize active

Christian participation in the process of awakening that our region needs today. We want to do this in ways that are relevant to our times. History testifies to centuries of Christian contribution to the social, political, and economic development and prosperity of the region, in the areas of education, health, culture, literature, journalism, arts and other fields.

3.2 We realize that the future of the Christians of the Middle East is tied closely to the future of the Middle East itself. We do not claim that there is a solution for Christians only, or that there is a magic recipe for the region as whole. Certainly, we do not presume that Christianity is the answer, just as we do not consider Islam to be the answer. In fact, we do not believe that there is a religious solution to the crisis that this region suffers. We believe, however, that religion holds lofty human values that can constitute an essential element for the progress and development of our societies. It would be an error, therefore, to ignore religious values that can build an individual as well as a society. We also recognize that religion can be misused, to divide and alienate rather than to bring people together. There is an enormous richness in the diversity of our region; and we salute a society that celebrates pluralism and cultural variety.

3.3 Therefore, we believe and stress that we have a positive and important role to play, since we have a calling in our homelands. Our history and geography give testimony to this. It is not a coincidence that our Bible, the rule of our faith and practice, was given through inspiration to our forebears, and was set down in writing by those godly saints. We fix our eyes upon the author and perfecter of our faith, Jesus Christ, who dwelt among us, and went about teaching and doing good in our midst and in these our lands. Indeed, Jesus Christ still calls us through his word, and by his example, to be witnesses to him and to his message, and to continue his ministry in word and deed here, today. It is here that we exist and are rooted. Our homelands have demands on us. We are committed to this calling. And we are loathe to ignore or run away from our duty.

4. We Believe, Therefore We Commit

4.1 We believe in One God, who created the universe and honored humankind, even making humans his vicegerents on earth, entrusting them to maintain and embellish this planet. Therefore, we are committed to caring for creation and to the responsible management of the earth's resources, as faithful stewards. We are also committed to guarding the dignity of all humankind, regardless of gender, ethnicity, religion or belief.

4.2 We believe in the One Triune God. Therefore, we are committed to working towards the unity and integrity of each of our nations and the harmony of its visions and goals. We do this while celebrating and preserving the rich and unique diversity in our countries.

4.3 We believe in God, omnipotent and all merciful, creator and sustainer of the universe, who did not abandon this world but is still active, creatively giving life and renewing it. Therefore, we are committed to remaining in our homelands and to being involved actively in their renewal and development, dedicating our gifts to creativity and innovation.

4.4 We believe in Jesus Christ, the incarnate Word of God, who dwelt among us, who taught, healed and went about doing good, calling all peoples to repentance and righteousness, and proclaiming liberty and goodness. Therefore, we are committed to following his path, and to continuing his mission in the service of humanity through the ministries of education, healing, development, culture and the arts. We do this as we also pursue justice, seek and make peace, and advocate human rights in our Arab context.

4.5 We believe in Jesus Christ who died on the cross and in the victory of his resurrection. He experienced the agony and hardships of human life, endured humiliation, and suffered the pain of injustice and persecution. He then rose triumphantly, proclaiming the dawn a new era. Therefore, we are committed to solidarity with those who are crushed, weak, and oppressed. We shall not give in to despair or to the logic of death; but will live with the power and hope of the resurrection, and in our conduct shall bear witness to the sanctity of life.

4.6 We believe in the Holy Spirit who works in us and through us, comforting us in our hardships, reviving and renewing our strengths. Therefore, we are committed to striving towards the renewal of our societies and their institutions, and will seek a humanity and a spirituality that enrich life and glorify its Giver.

4.7 We believe in one holy catholic and apostolic Church. Therefore, we are committed to the ecumenical spirit and to ecumenical work, to thinking, planning and acting together. We also extend our hands to our neighbors of other faiths, in order together to build just, secure, and free societies that embrace all their citizens.

4.8 We believe in the forgiveness of sins, and realize that we are often part of the problem instead of being part of the solution. Therefore, we are committed to accountability and self-correction, and to forgiving others as we have been forgiven, so that we may be part of establishing a new era for the peoples of this region.

4.9 We believe in God, the Supreme Judge, before whom we all shall stand one day to give an account for our lives. Therefore, we are committed to work diligently to assure that our countries have just constitutions, upright governments and fair laws. We dedicate ourselves to the task of ensuring that all citizens, without exception, have equal rights and obligations.

4.10 We believe in eternal life, and realize that people in our region believe in life after death, but are starting to despair of the possibility of life with dignity before death. Therefore, we are committed to strive toward ensuring a decent life for people in our time and place.

4.11 As we live through these difficult times in the history of our region, when Christians are suffering from persecution, demonization, and forced displacement, we realize that this calamity does not target just Christians, but countries as a whole. We also realize that there is no salvation in sight, nor will deliverance come effortlessly. It will come only as a result of a difficult process of labor pains – as in childbirth - and through a continuing and cumulative cultivation of awareness leading to a radical reformation of systems and mindsets, over many generations.

4.12 Despite all the difficult challenges, we are committed to remaining and persevering with those who share our concerns, through the process of awakening that our societies need. We are accountable before God, to acknowledge his commandment of seeking the good and well-being of our homelands, as we have a stake in their future.

4.13 This is our understanding and declaration of a conscientious and active faith, positive involvement, and active participation. Therefore...

We believe and commit.

End Notes:

1. See the website www.cafcaw.org for related material.

2. For more about Diyar Consortium, check: www.diyar.ps and www.daralkalima.edu.ps

3. Diyar Consortium published a book documenting some of the issues discussed during the first launching phase of the Religion and State – Middle East project under the title: **"Religion and State: Theology, Women and the Media"**, as part of the Civil Society Series, edited by Mitri Raheb, Bethlehem, Palestine, Diyar Publisher, 2011. An additional book is: **"Religion and State: The Example of Jordan"** (Amman: The Center of Jerusalem for Political Studies, 2010, in cooperation with the International Center of Bethlehem (ICB) and the Olof Palme International Center in Sweden).

4. In preparation for this document, we have done careful, in-depth study and analysis, and were guided by several documents issued by prominent institutions and which were relevant to our subject. Those include: **"The Declaration by Al-Azhar and the Intellectuals (on the legal ordinances of fundamental freedoms)"**, Office of Sheikh Al-Azhar al-Sharif, Cairo, 2012; **"The Arab Social Charter"** of the Arab Thought Forum, Amman, Jordan, January 2012; the Document of 138 Scholars: **"A Common Word"** of the Royal Aal al-Bayt Institute for Islamic Thought, Amman, Jordan, 2007, in line with the Vatican Document (**"The Catholic Church in the Middle East: Communion and Witness"** – *"Ecclesia in Medio Oriente"*) published by the Special Assembly for the Middle East of the Synod of Bishops, the Vatican, 2010; as well as various resources on the Middle East issued by the World Council of Churches; and the **"Christians Presence and Witness in the Middle East"** statement issued by the Middle East Council of Churches, Beirut, Lebanon, 2012. We are also in ongoing consultation with prominent figures and partners, individually as well as institutionally, who have valuable insight and knowledge on the issues.

5. What distinguishes this from other documents is that it entails a "General Framework for Action" with guidelines for the two coming years 2015-2016 that is already in place. The guidelines are based on the foundations and values of our faith, as well as on our persistence to contribute effectively to our societies.

6. In earlier studies (**"Religion and State: Theology, Women and the Media,"** p. 8-9) we were introduced to several problems raised by the following ques-

tions that would define the measurements of the relation between religion and state in the Arab World:

- Is the state neutral with regards to religion, or does it practice favoritism or differentiate between religions? Does it harass religious groups? How is the relationship between religion and state regulated?

- Does the constitution specify a particular religion, and if so, what about other religions?

- Is there violation of religious freedom, or any harassment or mistreatment to religious communities?

- Does the state interfere in the religious legislations?

- Are there laws that protect the freedom of the believer, which would include the right to convert to another religion or to renounce religion? Are there civic alternatives that are not related to religious bodies?

- To what extent do religious groups interfere in the policies of government, and what is their influence on the systems within the state?

7. This area ranks the lowest when it comes to the subject of separation of religion and state (*op. cit.*, 10). Moreover, the region has recently been suffering from a kind of hysteria to develop religious states, whether Muslim or Jewish, which is discriminatory against people from other religions, and this is deeply rooted in the history of the region.

- In all twenty Arab states of the Middle East, there is no separation between religion and state.

- Seventeen (17) of these twenty countries declare that the religion of the state is Islam.

- Nineteen (19) of these countries forbid evangelization, and fourteen (14) of them criminalize conversion.

- Twelve (12) of these countries ban any publication by a religious minority group,

- Fifteen (15) prohibit the formation of religious parties, and ten (10) track fundamental leaders.

- Six (6) countries forbid minority religions, and one (1) country does not allow the practice of any other religion. This subject should not be looked at apart from the general context, which reflects the absence of democracy, modernity, and productivity in all of its different aspects, as well as the phenomenon of polarization between the autocratic governments and the religious streams; all of which aims at gaining political control, and is essentially indifferent to the legitimacy of Human Rights.

8. *Towards Freedom in the Arab World: Arab Human Development Report 2004*, United Nations Development Program, 2004.

9. *Challenges to Human Security in the Arab Countries: The Arab Human Development Report 2009,* the United Nations Development Program, 2009.

10. Hassan R. Hammoud. *Illiteracy in the Arab World,* prepared in 2005 and published by UNSCO in 2006.

11. *Towards the Rise of Women in the Arab World: The Arab Human Development Report 2005*; the United Nations Development Program, 2005.

12. *Creating Opportunities for Future Generations: The Arab Human Development Report 2002*; the United Nations Development Program, 2002.

13. Here we need to point out to some important statements, prominent among which is the declaration by Al-Azhar Al-Sharif **"On Combatting Extremism and Terrorism"** issued on December 4, 2014, (www.azhar.eg/conf2014). There are also other writings by Muslim scholars, such as Dr. Mohammed Al-Sammak's op-ed titled **"A Call for an Islamic Initiative against Terrorism and Extremism,"** Beirut, the Lebanese daily, *al-Mustaqbal*, No.5123, August 18, 2014, p. 19. (http://www.almustaqbal.com/v4/article.aspx?Type=NP&ArticleID=62857) And also: **"An Islamic Response to the Patriarchs Council Statement"**, Beirut, *Al-Safir* newspaper, August 29, 2014. (http://assafir.com/article/2/369067)

14. *Building a Knowledge Society: Arab Human Development Report 2003;* the United Nations Development Program, 2003.

4 December 2014

www.ingramcontent.com/pod-product-compliance
Lightning Source LLC
Chambersburg PA
CBHW072024290526
45787CB00014B/1859